William [illegible]

For Chas
from Allen

Charles [illegible]
New York
1941

THE MODERN LIBRARY

OF THE WORLD'S BEST BOOKS

THE ART OF AUBREY BEARDSLEY

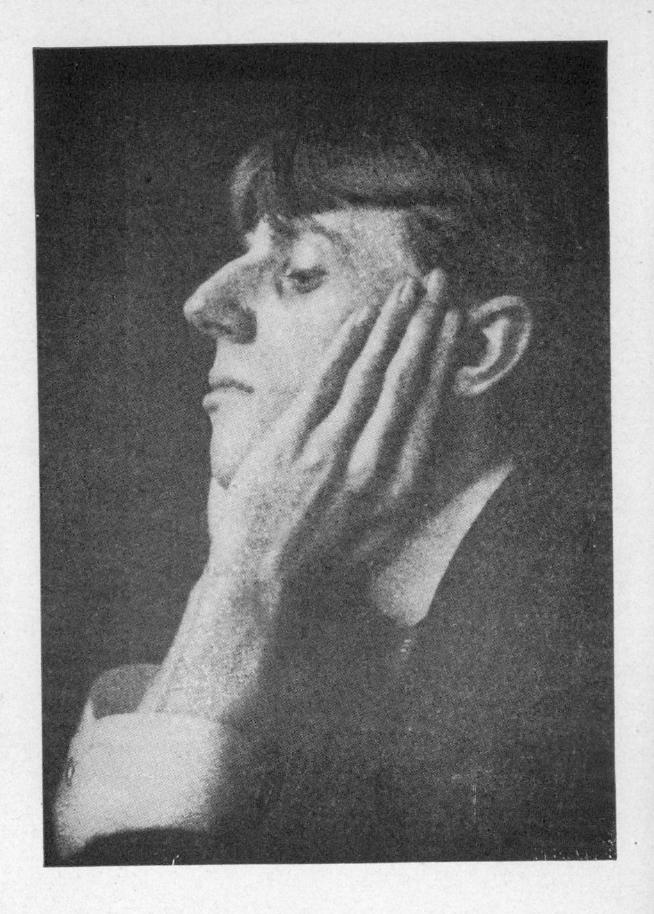

Aubrey Beardsley.

THE ART OF AUBREY BEARDSLEY

Introduction by ARTHUR SYMONS

THE MODERN LIBRARY

PUBLISHERS : NEW YORK

Manufactured in the United States of America
Bound for THE MODERN LIBRARY *by H. Wolff*

CONTENTS

ILLUSTRATIONS

ILLUSTRATIONS

AUBREY BEARDSLEY
AN ESSAY WITH A PREFACE

BY

ARTHUR SYMONS

PREFACE

IT was in the summer of 1895 that I first met Aubrey Beardsley. A publisher had asked me to form and edit a new kind of magazine, which was to appeal to the public equally in its letterpress and its illustrations: need I say that I am defining the *"Savoy"?* It was, I admit, to have been something of a rival to the "*Yellow Book*," which had by that time ceased to mark a movement, and had come to be little more than a publisher's magazine. I forget exactly when the expulsion of Beardsley from the "*Yellow Book*" had occurred; it had been sufficiently recent, at all events, to make Beardsley singularly ready to fall in with my project when I went to him and asked him to devote himself to illustrating my quarterly. He was supposed, just then, to be dying; and as I entered the room, and saw him lying out on a couch, horribly white, I wondered if I had come too late. He was full of ideas, full of enthusiasm, and I think it was then that he suggested the name "*Savoy*," finally adopted after endless changes and uncertainties.

A little later we met again at Dieppe, where for a month I saw him daily. It was at Dieppe that the "*Savoy*" was really planned, and it was in the café which Mr. Sickert has so often painted that I wrote the slightly pettish and defiant "Editorial Note," which made so many enemies for the first number. Dieppe just then was a meeting-place for the younger generation; some of us spent the whole summer there, lazily but profitably; others came and went. Beardsley at that time imagined himself to be unable to draw anywhere but in London. He made one or two faint attempts, and even prepared a canvas for a picture which was never painted, in the hospitable studio in which M. Jacques Blanche painted the admirable portrait reproduced in the frontispiece. But he found many subjects, some of which he afterwards worked out, in the expressive opportunities of the Casino and the beach. He never walked; I never saw him look at the sea; but at night he was almost always to be seen watching the gamblers at *petits chevaux*, studying them with a sort of hypnotised attention for that picture of "*The Little Horses*," which was never done. He liked the large, deserted rooms, at hours when no one was there; the sense of frivolous things caught at a moment of suspended life, *en déshabille*. He would glance occasionally, but with more impatience, at the dances, especially the children's dances, in the concert room; but he rarely missed a concert, and would glide in every afternoon, and sit on the high benches at the side, always carrying his large, gilt-leather portfolio with the magnificent, old, red-lined folio paper, which he would often open, to write some lines in pencil. He was at work then, with an almost pathetic tenacity, at his story, never to be finished, the story which never could have been finished, "*Under the Hill*," a new version, a parody (like Laforgue's parodies, but how unlike them, or anything!) of the story of Venus and Tannhäuser. Most of it was done at these concerts, and in the little, close writing-room, where visitors sat writing letters. The fragment published in the first two numbers of the "*Savoy*" had passed through many stages before it found its way there, and would have passed through more if it had ever been carried further. Tannhäuser, not quite willingly, had put on Abbé's disguise, and there were other unwilling disguises in those brilliant, disconnected, fantastic pages, in which every sentence was meditated over, written for its own sake, and left to find its way in its own paragraph. It could never have been finished, for it had never really been begun; but what undoubted, singular, literary ability there is in it, all the same!

I think Beardsley would rather have been a great writer than a great artist; and I remember, on one occasion, when he had to fill up a form of admission to some library to which I was introducing him, his insistence on describing himself as "man of letters." At one time he was going to write an essay on "*Les Liaisons*

Dangereuses," at another he had planned a book on Rousseau. But his plans for writing changed even more quickly than his plans for doing drawings, and with less profitable results in the meantime. He has left no prose except that fragment of a story; and in verse only the three pieces published in the "*Savoy.*" Here, too, he was terribly anxious to excel; and his patience over a medium so unfamiliar, and hence so difficult, to him as verse, was infinite. We spent two whole days on the grassy ramparts of the old castle at Arques-la-Bataille, near Dieppe; I working at something or other in one part, he working at "*The Three Musicians*" in another. The eight stanzas of that amusing piece of verse are really, in their own way, a *tour de force;* by sheer power of will, by deliberately saying to himself, "I will write a poem," and by working with such strenuous application that at last a certain result, the kind of result he had willed, did really come about, he succeeded in doing what he had certainly no natural aptitude for doing. How far was that more genuine aspect of his genius also an "infinite capacity for taking pains?"

The republication by Mr. Lane, the publisher of the "*Yellow Book,*" of Beardsley's contributions in prose and verse to the "*Savoy,*" its "rival," as Mr. Lane correctly calls it, with the illustrations which there accompanied them, reopens a little, busy chapter in contemporary history. It is the history of yesterday, and it seems already at this distance of half a century. Then, what brave petulant outbursts of poets and artists, what comic rivalries and reluctances of publishers, what droll conflicts of art and morality, what thunders of the trumpets of the press! The press is silent now, or admiring; the publishers have changed places, and all rivalries are handsomely buried, with laudatory inscriptions on their tombstones. The situation has its irony, which would have appealed most to the actor most conspicuously absent from the scene.

Beardsley was very anxious to be a writer, and, though in his verse there was no merit except that of a thing done to order, to one's own order, and done without a flaw in the process, there was, in his prose, a much finer quality, and his fragment of an unachieved and unplanned romance has a savour of its own. It is the work, not of a craftsman, but of an amateur, and in this it may be compared with the prose of Whistler, so great an artist in his own art and so brilliant an amateur in the art of literature. Beardsley too was something of a wit, and in his prose one sees hard intellect, untinged with sentiment, employed on the work of fancy. He wrote and he saw, unimaginatively, and without passion, but with a fierce sensitive precision; and he saw by preference things elaborately perverse, full of fantastic detail, unlikely and possible things, brought toegther from the four corners of the universe. All those descriptions in "Under the Hill" are the equivalent of his drawings, and they are of especial interest in showing how definitely he saw things, and with what calm minuteness he could translate what seemed a feverish drawing into oddly rational words. Listen, for instance, to this garden-picture: "In the middle was a huge bronze fountain with three basins. From the first rose a many-breasted dragon and four little loves mounted upon swans, and each love was furnished with a bow and arrow. Two of them that faced the monster seemed to recoil in fear, two that were behind made bold enough to aim their shafts at him. From the verge of the second sprang a circle of slim golden columns that supported silver doves with tails and wings spread out. The third, held by a group of grotesquely attenuated satyrs, is centred with a thin pipe hung with masks and roses and capped with children's heads." The picture was never drawn, but does it want more than the drawing?

The prose of *"Under the Hill"* does not arrive at being really good prose, but it has felicities that astonish, those felicities by which the amateur astonishes the craftsman. The imaginary dedication is the best, the most sustained, piece of writing in it, but there is wit everywhere, subtly intermingled with fancy, and there are touches of color such as this: "Huge moths, so richly winged that they must have banqueted upon tapestries and royal stuffs, slept on the pillars that flanked either side of the gateway, and the eyes of all the moths remained open and were burning and bursting with a mesh of veins." Here and there is a thought or a mental sensation like that of "the irritation of loveliness that can never be entirely comprehended, or ever enjoyed to the utmost." There are many affectations, some copied from Oscar Wilde, others personal enough, such as the use of French words instead of English ones: "chevelure" for hair, and "pantoufles" for slippers. I do not think that Beardsley finally found a place for the word which he had adapted from the French, "papillions," instead of "papillons" or butterflies; it would have come amusingly, and it was one of his pet words. But his whole conception of writing was that of a game with words; some obsolete game with a quaint name, like that other favorite word of his, "spellicans," for which he did find a place in the story.

Taken literally, this fragment is hardly more than a piece of nonsense, and was hardly meant to be more than that. Yet, beyond the curiosity and ingenuity of the writing, how much there is of real skill in the evocation of a certain impossible but quite credible atmosphere! Its icy artificiality is indeed one of its qualities, and produces, by mere negation, an emotional effect. Beardsley did not believe in his own enchantments, was never haunted by his own terrors, and, in his queer sympathy and familiarity with evil, had none of the ardors of a lost soul. In the place of Faust he would have kept the devil at his due distance by a polite incredulity, openly expressed, as to the very existence of his interlocutor.

It was on the balcony of the Hotel Henri IV, at Arques, one of those September evenings, that I had the only quite serious, almost solemn, conversation I ever had with Beardsley. Not long before we had gone together to visit Alexandre Dumas *fils* at Puy, and it was from talking of that thoughtful, but entirely, Parisian writer, and his touching, in its unreal way so real, "Dame aux Camélias" (the novel, not the play), which Beardsley admired so much, that we passed into an unexpectedly intimate mood of speculation. Those stars up yonder, whether they were really the imprisoning worlds of other creatures like ourselves; the strange ways by which the soul might have come and must certainly go; death, and the future: it was such things that I found him speaking, for once without mockery. And he told me then a singular dream or vision which he had had when a child, waking up at night in the moonlight and seeing a great crucifix, with a bleeding Christ, falling off the wall, where certainly there was not, and had never been, any crucifix. It is only by remembering that one conversation, that vision, the tone of awe with which he told it, that I can, with a great effort, imagine to myself the Beardsley whom I knew with his so positive intelligence. his imaginative sight of the very spirit of man as a thing of definite outline, transformed finally into the Beardsley who died in the peace of the last sacraments of the Church, holding the rosary between his fingers.

And yet, if you read carefully the book of letters to an unnamed friend, which has been published six years after his death, it will be seen that here too, as always, we are in the presence of a real thing. In these naked letters we see a man die. And the man dies inch by inch, like one who slips inch by inch over a precipice, and knows that the grasses at which his fingers tear, clutching their feeble roots, are but delaying him for so many instants, and that he must soon fall. We see a fine, clear-sighted intellect set on one problem: how to get well; then, how to get a little better; and then, how not to get worse. He records the weather of each day, and each symptom of his disease; with a desperate calmness, which but rarely deserts or betrays him. To-day he feels better and can read Laclos; to-morrow he is not so well, and he must hear no music, He has pious books and pious friends for the days when he is driven back upon himself, and must turn aside his attention from suffering which brings despair. Nothing exists any longer, outside himself; and there may be safety somewhere, in a "preservative girdle" or in a friend's prayer. He asks for both. Both are to keep him alive. He meets at Mentone someone who seems worse than himself, and who yet "lives on and does things. My spirits have gone up immensely since I have known him." A change of sky, the recurrence of a symptom: "to-day, alas, there is a downpour and I am miserably depressed." He reads S. Alphonsus Liguori, and it is "mere physical exhaustion more than hardness of heart that leaves me so apathetic and uninterested." He clings to religion as to his friend, thinking that it may help him to keep himself in life. He trains himself to be gentle, to hope little, to attack the sources of health stealthily. A "wonderful stretch of good health," a few whole days of it, makes him "tremble at moments." "Don't think me foolish to haggle about a few months," he writes, when he is hoping, all the time, that "the end is less near than it seems." He is received into the Church, makes his first confession, makes his first communion. It seems to him that each is a new clutch upon the roots of the grasses.

The whole book is a study in fear, and by its side everything else that has been done, imaginatively or directly, on that fierce passion, seems mere oratory or a talking beside the question. Here Beardsley is, as he is in his drawings, close, absorbed, limited, and unflinching. That he should be so honest with his fear; that he should sit down before its face and study it feature by feature; that he should never turn aside his eyes for more than an instant, make no attempt to escape, but sit at home with it, travel with it, see it in his mirror, taste it with the sacrament: that is the marvellous thing, and the sign of his fundamental sincerity in life and art.

AUBREY BEARDSLEY

ANIMA naturaliter pagana, Aubrey Beardsley ended a long career, at the age of twenty-six, in the arms of the Church. No artist of our time, none certainly whose work has been in black and white, has reached a more universal, or a more contested fame; none has formed himself, out of such alien elements, a more personal originality of manner; none has had so wide an influence on contemporary art. He had the fatal speed of those who are to die young; that disquieting completeness and extent of knowledge, that absorption of a lifetime in an hour, which we find in those who hasten to have done their work before noon, knowing that they will not see the evening. He had played the piano in drawing-rooms as an infant prodigy, before, I suppose, he had ever drawn a line: famous at twenty as a draughtsman, he found time, in those incredibly busy years which remained to him, to deliberately train himself into a writer of prose which was, in its way, as original as his draughtsmanship, and into a writer of verse which had at least ingenious and original moments. He seemed to have read everything, and had his preferences as adroitly in order, as wittily in evidence, as almost any man of letters; indeed, he seemed to know more, and was a sounder critic, of books than of pictures; with perhaps a deeper feeling for music than for either. His conversation had a peculiar kind of brilliance different in order but scarcely inferior in quality to that of any other contemporary master of that art; a salt, whimsical dogmatism, equally full of convinced egoism and of imperturbable keen-sightedness. Generally choosing to be paradoxical; and vehement on behalf of any enthusiasm of the mind, he was the dupe of none of his own statements, or indeed of his own enthusiasms, and, really, very coldly impartial. I scarcely except even his own judgment of himself in spite of his petulant, amusing self-assertion, so full of the childishness of genius. He thought, and was right in thinking, very highly of himself; he admired himself enormously; but his intellect would never allow itself to be deceived even about his own accomplishments.

This clear, unemotional intellect, emotional only in the perhaps highest sense, where emotion almost ceases to be recognizable, in the abstract, for ideas, for lines, left him with all his interests in life, with all his sociability, of a sort essentially very lonely. Many people were devoted to him, but he had, I think, scarcely a friend, in the fullest sense of the word; and I doubt if there were more than one or two people for whom he felt any real affection. In spite of constant ill-health he had an astonishing tranquility of nerves; and it was doubtless that rare quality which kept him, after all, alive so long. How far he had deliberately acquired command over his nerves and his emotions, as he deliberately acquired command over brain and hand, I do not know. But there it certainly was, one of the bewildering characteristics of so contradictory a temperament.

One of his poses, as people say, one of those things, that is, in which he was most sincere, was his care in outwardly conforming to the conventions which make for elegance and restraint; his necessity of dressing well, of showing no sign of the professional artist. He had a great contempt for, what seemed to inferior craftsmen, inspiration, for what I have elsewhere called the plenary inspiration of first thoughts; and he hated the outward and visible signs of an inward yeastiness and incoherency. It amused him to denounce everything, certainly, which Baudelaire would have denounced; and, along with some mere *gaminerie,* there was a very serious and adequate theory of art at the back of all his destructive criticisms. It was a profound thing which he said to a friend of mine who asked him whether he ever saw visions: "No," he replied, "I do not allow myself to see them except on paper." All his art is in that phrase.

And he attained, to the full, one certainly of his many desires, and that one, perhaps, of which he was most keenly or most continuously conscious: contemporary fame of a popular singer or a professional beauty, the fame of Yvette Guilbert or of Cléo de Mérode. And there was logic in his insistence on this point, in his eagerness after immediate and clamorous success. Others might have waited; he knew that he had not the time to wait. After all, posthumous fame is not a very cheering prospect to look forward to, on the part of those who have worked without recompense, if the pleasure or the relief of work is not enough in itself. Every artist has his own secret, beyond the obvious one, of why he works, it is generally some unhappiness, some dissatisfaction with the things about one, some too desperate or too contemptuous sense of the meaning of existence. At one period of his life a man works at his art to please a woman; then he works because he is tired of pleasing her. Work for the work's sake it always must be, in a profound sense; and, with Beardsley, not less certainly than with Blake or with Rosetti. But that other, that accidental, significant motive, was, with Beardsley, the desire to fill his few working years with the immediate echo of a great notoriety.

Like most artists who have thought much of popularity he had an immense contempt for the public; and the desire to kick that public into admiration, and then to kick it for admiring the wrong thing or not knowing why it was admiring, led him into many of his most outrageous practical jokes of the pen. He was partly right and partly wrong, for he was indiscriminate; and to be indiscriminate is always to be partly right and partly wrong. The wish to *épater le bourgeois* is a natural one, and, though a little beside the question, does not necessarily lead one astray. The general public, of course, does not in the least know why it admires the right thing to-day though it admired the wrong thing yesterday. But there is such a thing as denying your Master while you are rebuking a servant-girl. Beardsley was without the very sense of respect; it was one of his limitations.

And this limitation was an unfortunate one, for it limited his ambition. With the power of creating beauty, which should be pure beauty, he turned aside, only too often, to that lower kind of beauty which is the mere beauty of technique in a composition otherwise meaningless, trivial, or grotesque. Saying to himself, "I can do what I like; there is nothing I could not do if I chose to, if I chose to take the trouble; but why should I offer hard gold when an I.O.U. will be just the same? I can pay up whenever the money is really wanted," he allowed himself to be content with what he knew would startle, doing it with infinite pains, to his own mind conscientiously, but doing it with that lack of reverence for great work which is one of the most sterlizing characteristics of the present day.

The epithet *fin de siècle* has been given, somewhat loosely, to a great deal of modern French art, and to art which, in one way or another, seems to attach itself to contemporary France. Out of the great art of Manet, the serious art of Degas, the exquisite art of Whistler, all, in such different ways, so modern, there has come into existence a new, very modern, very far from great or serious or really exquisite kind of art, which has expressed itself largely in the "Courrier Français," the "Gil Blas Illustré," and the posters. All this art may be said to be what the quite new art of the poster certainly is, art meant for the street, for people who are walking fast. It comes into competition with the newspapers, with the music-halls; half contemptuously, it popularises itself; and, with real qualities and a real measure of good intention, finds itself forced to seek for sharp, sudden, arresting means of expression. Instead of seeking pure beauty, the seriousness and self-absorption of great art, it takes, wilfully and for effect, that beauty which is least evident, indeed least genuine; nearest to ugliness in the grotesque, nearest to triviality in a certain elegant daintiness, nearest also to brutality and the spectacular vices. Art is not sought for its own sake, but the manual craftsman perfects himself to express a fanciful, ingenious, elaborate, somewhat tricky way of seeing things, which he has deliberately adopted. It finds its own in the eighteenth century, so that Willette becomes a kind of petty, witty Watteau of Montmartre; it parodies the art of stained glass, with Grasset and his followers; it juggles with iron bars and masses of shadow, like Lautrec. And, in its direct assault on the nerves, it pushes naughtiness to obscenity, deforms observation into caricature, dexterity of line and handling being cultivated as one cultivates a particular, deadly *botte* in fencing.

And this art, this art of the day and hour, competes not merely with the appeal and the popularity of the theatrical spectacle, but directly with theatrical methods, the methods of stage illusion. The art of the ballet counts for much, in the evolution of many favorite effects of contemporary drawing, and not merely because Degas has drawn dancers, with his reserved, essentially classical mastery of form. By its rapidity of flight within bounds, by its bird-like and flower-like caprices of color and motion, by that appeal to the imagination which comes from its silence (to which music is but like an accompanying shadow, so closely, so discreetly, does it follow the feet of the dancers), by its appeal to the eyes and to the senses, its adorable artificiality, the ballet has tempted almost every draughtsman, as the interiors of music-halls have also been singularly tempting, with their extraordinary tricks of light, their suddenness of gesture, their triumphant tinsel, their fantastic humanity. And pantomime, too, in the French and correct, rather than in the

English and incorrect, sense of that word, has had its significant influence. In those pathetic gaieties of Willette, in the windy laughter of the frivolities of Chéret, it is the masquerade, the English clown or acrobat seen at the Folies-Bergère, painted people mimicking puppets, who have begotten this masquerading humanity of posters and illustrated papers. And the point of view is the point of view of Pierrot—

> "le subtil génie
> De sa malice infinie
> De poète-grimacier"—

Verlaine's *Pierrot gamin.*

Pierrot is one of the types we live, or of the moment, perhaps, out of which we are just passing. Pierrot is passionate; but he does not believe in great passions. He feels himself to be sickening with a fever, or else perilously convalescent; for love is a disease, which he is too weak to resist or endure. He has worn his heart on his sleeve so long, that it has hardened in the cold air. He knows that his face is powdered, and, if he sobs, it is without tears; and it is hard to distinguish, under the chalk, if the grimace which twists his mouth awry is more laughter or mockery. He knows that he is condemned to be always in public, that emotion would be supremely out of keeping with his costume, that he must remember to be fantastic if he would not be merely ridiculous. And so he becomes exquisitely false, dreading above all things that "one touch of nature" which would ruffle his disguise, and leave him defenceless. Simplicity, in him, being the most laughable thing in the world, he becomes learned, perverse, intellectualising his pleasures, brutalising his intellect; his mournful contemplation of things becoming a kind of grotesque joy, which he expresses in the only symbols at his command, tracing his Giotto's O with the elegance of his pirouette.

And Beardsley, with almost more than the Parisian's deference to Paris, and to the moment, was, more than any Parisian, this *Pierrot gamin*. He was more than that, but he was that: to be that was part of what he learnt from France. It helped him to the pose which helped him to reveal himself; as Burne-Jones had helped him when he did the illustrations to the "Morte d'Arthur," (Ill. 7-10) as Japanese art helped him to free himself from that influence, as Eisen and Saint-Aubin showed him the way to the "Rape of the Lock." (Ill. 53) He had that originality which surrenders to every influence, yet surrenders to absorb, not to be absorbed; that originality which, constantly shifting, is true always to its centre. Whether he learnt from M. Grasset or from Mr. Ricketts, from an 1830 fashion-plate, or from an engraved plate by Hogarth, whether the scenery of Arques-la-Bataille composed itself into a pattern in his mind, or, in the Casino at Dieppe, he made a note of the design of a looped-up window-blind, he was always drawing to himself, out of the order of art or the confusion of natural things, the thing he wanted, the thing he could make his own. And he found, in the French art of the moment, a joyous sadness, the service to God of Mephistopheles, which his own temperament and circumstances were waiting to suggest to him.

"In more ways than one do men sacrifice to the rebellious angels," says St. Augustine; and Beardsley's sacrifice, together with that of all great decadent art, the art of Rops or the art of Baudelaire, is really a sacrifice to the eternal beauty, and only seemingly to the powers of evil. And here let me say that I have no concern with what neither he nor I could have had absolute knowledge of, his own intention in his work. A man's intention, it must be remembered, from the very fact that it is conscious, is much less intimately himself than the sentiment which his work conveys to me. So large is the sub-conscious element in all artistic creation, that I should have doubted whether Beardsley himself knew what he intended to do, in this or that really significant drawing. Admitting that he could tell exactly what he had intended, I should be quite prepared to show that he had really done the very contrary.

Thus when I say he was a profoundly spiritual artist, though seeming to care chiefly for the manual part of his work; that he expresses evil with an intensity which lifted it into a region almost of asceticism, though attempting, not seldom, little more than a joke or a caprice in line; and that he was above all, though almost against his own will, a satirist who has seen the ideal; I am putting forward no paradox, nothing really contradictory, but a simple analysis of the work as it exists.

At times he attains pure beauty, has the unimpaired vision; in the best of the Salomé" (Ills. 15-29) designs, here and there afterwards. From the first it is a diabolic beauty, but it is not yet divided against itself. The consciousness of sin is always there, but it is sin first transfigured by beauty, and then disclosed by beauty; sin, conscious of itself, of its inability to escape itself, and showing in its ugliness the law it has broken. His world is a world of phantoms, in which the desire of the perfecting of mortal sensations, a desire of infinity, has overpassed mortal limits, and poised them, so faint, so quivering, so passionate for flight, in a hopeless and strenuous immobility. They have the sensitiveness of the spirit, and that bodily sensitiveness which wastes their veins and imprisons them in the attitude of their luxurious meditation. They are too thoughtful to be ever really simple, or really absorbed by either flesh or spirit. They have nothing of what is "healthy" or merely "animal" in their downward course towards repentance; no overwhelming passion hurries them beyond themselves; they do not capitulate to an open assault of the enemy of souls. It is the soul in them that sins, sorrowfully, without reluctance, inevitably. Their bodies are faint and eager with wantonness; they desire more pleasure than there is in the world, fiercer and more exquisite pains, a more intolerable suspense. They have put off the common burdens of humanity, and put on that loneliness which is the rest of saints and the unrest of those who have sinned with the intellect. They are a little lower than the angels, and they walk between these and the fallen angels, without part or lot in the world.

Here, then, we have a sort of abstract spiritual corruption, revealed in beautiful form; sin transfigured by beauty. And here, even if we go no further, is an art intensely spiritual, an art in which evil purifies itself by its own intensity, and the beauty which transfigures it. The one thing in the world which is without hope is that mediocrity which is the sluggish content of inert matter. Better be vividly awake to evil than, in mere somnolence, close the very issues and approaches of good and evil. For evil itself, carried to the point of a perverse ecstasy, becomes a kind of good, by means of that energy which, otherwise directed, is virtue; and which can never, no matter how its course may be changed, fail to retain something of its original efficacy. The devil is nearer to God, by the whole height from which he fell, than the average man who has not recognised his own need to rejoice or to repent. And so a profound spiritual corruption, instead of being a more "immortal" thing than the gross and pestiferous humanity of Hogarth or of Rowlandson, is more nearly, in the final and abstract sense, moral, for it is the triumph of the spirit over the flesh, to no matter what end. It is a form of divine possession, by which the inactive and materialising soul is set in fiery motion, lured from the ground, into at least a certain high liberty. And so we find evil justified of itself, and an art consecrated to the revelation of evil equally justified; its final justification being that declared by Plotinus, in his treatise "On the Nature of Good and Evil:" "But evil is permitted to remain by itself alone on account of the superior power and nature of good; because it appears from necessity everywhere comprehended and bound, in beautiful bands, like men fettered with golden chains, lest it should be produced openly to the views of divinity, or lest mankind should always behold its horrid shape when perfectly naked; and such is the supervening power of good, that whenever a glimpse of perfect evil is obtained we are immediately recalled to the memory of good by the image of the beautiful with which evil is invested."

In those drawings of Beardsley which are grotesque rather than beautiful, in which now all the beauty takes refuge, is itself a moral judgment. Look at that drawing called "The Scarlet Pastorale."* In front, a bloated harlequin struts close to the footlights, outside the play, on which he turns his back; beyond, sacramental candles have been lighted, and are guttering down in solitude, under an unseen wind. And between, on the sheer darkness of the stage, a bald and plumed Pierrot, holding in his vast, collapsing paunch with a mere rope of roses, shows the cloven foot, while Pierrette points at him in screaming horror, and the fat dancer turns on her toes indifferently. Need we go further to show how much more than Gautier's meaning lies in the old paradox of "Mademoiselle de Maupin," that "perfection of line is virtue?" That line which rounds the deformity of the cloven-footed sin, the line itself, is at once the revelation and the condemnation of vice, for it is part of that artistic logic which is morality.

Beardsley is the satirist of an age without convictions, and he can but paint hell as Baudelaire did, without pointing for contrast to any contemporary paradise. He employs the same rhetoric as Baudelaire, a method of emphasis which it is uncritical to think insecure. In that terrible annunciation of evil which he called "The Mysterious Rose-Garden," the lantern-bearing angel with winged sandals whispers, from among the falling roses, tidings of more than "pleasant sins." The leering dwarfs, the "monkeys," by which the mystics symbolised the earthlier vices; those immense bodies swollen with the lees of pleasure, and those cloaked and masked desires shuddering in gardens and smiling ambiguously at interminable toilets; are part of a symbolism which loses nothing by lack of emphasis. And the peculiar efficacy of this satire is that it is so much the satire of desire returning upon itself, the mockery of desire enjoyed, the mockery of desire denied. It is because he loves beauty that beauty's degradation obsesses him; it is because he is supremely conscious of virtue that vice has power to lay hold upon him. And, unlike those

* This drawing is not reproduced in this volume.

other acceptable satirists of our day, with whom satire exhausts itself in the rebuke of a drunkard leaning against a lamp-post, or a lady paying the wrong compliment in a drawing-room, he is the satirist of essential things; it is always the soul, and not the body's discontent only, which cries out of these insatiable eyes, that have looked on all their lusts, and out of these bitter mouths, that have eaten the dust of all their sweetness, and out of these hands, that have laboured delicately for nothing, and out of these feet, that have run after vanities. They are so sorrowful because they have seen beauty, and because they have departed from the line of beauty.

And after all, the secret of Beardsley is there; in the line itself rather than in anything, intellectually realised, which the line is intended to express. With Beardsley everything was a question of form: his interest in his work began when the paper was before him and the pen in his hand. And so, in one sense, he may be said never to have known what he wanted to do, while, in another, he knew very precisely indeed. He was ready to do, within certain limits, almost anything you suggested to him; as, when left to himself, he was content to follow the caprice of the moment. What he was sure of was his power of doing exactly what he proposed to himself to do; the thing itself might be "Salome" or "Belinda," "Ali Baba" or "Réjane," the "Morté d'Arthur" or the "Rheingold" or the "Liaisons Dangereuses;" the design might be for an edition of a classic or for the cover of a catalogue of second-hand books. And the design might seem to have no relation with the title of its subject, and, indeed, might have none: its relation was of line to line within the limits of its own border, and to nothing else in the world. Thus he could change his whole manner of working five or six times over in the course of as many years, seem to employ himself much of the time on trivial subjects, and yet retain, almost unimpaired, an originality which consisted in the extreme beauty and the absolute certainty of design.

It was a common error, at one time, to say that Beardsley could not draw. He certainly did not draw the human body with any attempt at rendering its own lines, taken by themselves; indeed, one of his latest drawings, an initial letter to "Volpone," is almost the first in which he has drawn a nude figure realistically. But he could draw, with extraordinary skill, in what is after all the essential way: he could make a line do what he wanted it to do, express the conception of form which it was his intention to express; and this is what the conventional draughtsman, Bouguereau, for instance, cannot do. The conventional draughtsman, any Academy student, will draw a line which shows quite accurately the curve of a human body, but all his science of drawing will not make you feel that line, will not make that line pathetic, as in the little, drooping body which a satyr and a Pierrot are laying in a puff-powder coffin, in the tail-piece to "Salomé." (Ill. 28.)

And then, it must never be forgotten, Beardsley was a decorative artist, and not anything else. From almost the very first he accepted convention; he set himself to see things as pattern. Taking freely all that the Japanese could give him, that release from the bondage of what we call real things, which comes to one man from an intense spirituality, to another from a consciousness of material form so intense that it becomes abstract, he made the world over again in his head, as if it existed only when it was thus re-made, and not even then, until it had been set down in black line on a white surface, in white line on a black surface. Working, as the decorative artist must work, in symbols almost as arbitrary, almost as fixed, as the squares of a chess-board, he swept together into his pattern all the incongruous things in the world, weaving them into congruity by his pattern. Using the puff-box, the toilet-table, the ostrich-feather hat, with a full consciousness of their suggestive quality in a drawing of archaic times, a drawing purposely fantastic, he put these things to beautiful uses, because he liked their forms, and because his space of white or black seemed to require some such arrangement of lines. They were the minims and crotchets by which he wrote down his music; they made the music, but they were not the music.

In the "Salomé" (Ills. 15-29) drawings, in most of the "Yellow Book" (Ills. 33, 34, 35, 37, 40, 41) drawings, we see Beardsley under this mainly Japanese influence; with, now and later, in his less serious work the but half-admitted influence of what was most actual, perhaps most temporary, in the French art of the day. *Pierrot gamin,* in "Salomé" itself, alternates, in such irreverences as the design of "The Black Cape," (Ill. 17) with the creator of the noble line, in the austere and terrible design of "The Climax," (Ill. 24) the ornate and vehement design of "The Peacock Skirt." (Ill. 16.) Here we get pure outline, as in the frontispiece; a mysterious intricacy, as in the border of the title-page and of the table of contents; a paradoxical beauty of mere wilfulness, but a wilfulness which has its meaning, its excuse, its pictorial justification, as in "The Toilette." (Ill. 22.) The "Yellow Book" and the first drawings for the "Savoy," (Ills. 54-57) a new influence has come into the work, the influence of the French eighteenth century. This influence, artificial as it is, draws him nearer, though somewhat unquietly nearer, to nature. Drawings like "The Fruit Bearers," in the first number of the "Savoy," with its solid and elaborate richness of ornament, or "The Coiffing," in the third number, with its delicate and elaborate grace, its witty concentration of line; drawings like the illustrations to the "Rape of the Lock," (Ill. 53) have, with less extravagance, and also a less strenuous intellectual effort, a new mastery of elegant form, not too far removed from nature while still subordinated to the effect of decoration, to the instinct of line. In the illustrations to Ernest Dowson's "Pierrot of the Minute," (Ills. 45-47) we have a more deliberate surrender, for the moment, to Eisen and Saint-Aubin, as yet another manner is seen working itself out. The illustrations to "Madamoiselle de Maupin," seemed to me, when I first saw them, with the exception of one extremely beautiful design in colour, to show a certain falling off in power, an actual weakness in the handling of the pen. But, in their not quite successful feeling after natural form, they did but represent, as I afterwards found, the moment of transition to what must now remain for us, and may well remain, Beardsley's latest manner. The four initial letters to "Volpone," the last of which was finished not more than three weeks before his death, have a new quality both of hand and of mind. They are done in pencil, and they lose, as such drawings are bound to lose, very greatly in the reduced reproduction. But, in the original, they are certainly, in sheer technical skill, equal to anything he had ever done, and they bring at the last, and with complete success, nature itself into the pattern. And here, under some solemn influence, the broken line of beauty has reunited; "the care is over," and the trouble has gone out of this no less fantastic world, in which Pan still smiles from his terminal column among the trees, but without the old malice. Human and animal form reassert themselves, with a new dignity, under this new respect for their capabilities. Beardsley has accepted the convention of nature itself, turning it to his own uses, extracting from it his own symbols, but no longer rejecting it for a convention entirely of his own making. And thus in his last work, done under the very shadow of death, we find new possibilities for an art, conceived as pure line, conducted through mere pattern, which, after many hesitations, has resolved finally upon the great compromise, that compromise which the greatest artists have made, between the mind's outline and the outline of visible things.

ILLUSTRATIONS

BY

AUBREY BEARDSLEY

THE LITANY OF MARY MAGDALEN

A PORTRAIT OF AUBREY BEARDSLEY, BY HIMSELF

INCIPIT VITA NOVA

SANDRO BOTTICELLI

" SIEGFRIED "
From " The Studio "

MERLIN
From " Le Morte d'Arthur "

VIGNETTE
From " Le Morte d'Arthur "

LA BEALE ISOUD AT JOYOUS GARDEN
From "Le Morte d'Arthur"

HOW QUEEN GUENEVER MADE HER A NUN
From "Le Morte d'Arthur"

"OF A NEOPHYTE, AND HOW THE BLACK ART WAS REVEALED UNTO HIM"

THE KISS OF JUDAS

A SUGGESTED REFORM IN BALLET COSTUME

BARON VERDIGRIS

THE WOMAN IN THE MOON
From " Salome "

THE PEACOCK SKIRT
From " Salome "

THE BLACK CAPE
From " Salome "

THE PLATONIC LAMENT
From " Salome "

ENTER HERODIAS
From " Salome "

THE EYES OF HEROD
From " Salome "

THE STOMACH DANCE
From "Salome"

THE TOILETTE OF SALOME
From " Salome "

THE DANCER'S REWARD
From " Salome "

THE CLIMAX
From " Salome "

THE TOILETTE OF SALOME, FIRST DRAWING
From " Salome "

JOHN AND SALOME
From " Salome "

SALOME ON SETTEE

DESIGN FOR TAILPIECE
From " Salome "

DESIGN FOR "SALOME"
From "The Studio"

DESIGN FOR COVER OF "THE YELLOW BOOK" PROSPECTUS

NIGHT PIECE

PORTRAIT OF MRS. PATRICK CAMPBELL

TITLE PAGE ORNAMENT FOR "THE YELLOW BOOK,"
VOLUME II

COMEDY BALLET OF MARIONETTES. I
From " The Yellow Book," Vol. II

COMEDY BALLET OF MARIONETTES. II
From "The Yellow Book," Vol. II

COMEDY BALLET OF MARIONETTES. III

GARCONS DE CAFE
From " The Yellow Book," Vol. II

THE SLIPPERS OF CINDERELLA

PORTRAIT OF MANTEGNA
From "The Yellow Book," Vol. III

THE WAGNERITES
From "The Yellow Book," Vol. III

LA DAME AUX CAMELIAS
From "The Yellow Book," Vol. III

MADAME REJANE

PORTRAIT OF BALZAC

DESIGN FOR FRONTISPIECE TO "AN EVIL MOTHER-HOOD"

DESIGN FOR FRONT COVER OF "PIERROT"

DESIGN FOR END-PAPER OF "PIERROT"

DESIGN FOR END-PAPER OF "PIERROT"

LYSISTRATA

AN ATHENIAN WOMAN

MYRRHINA

THE DREAM

THE BARON'S PRAYER

THE RAPE OF THE LOCK

DESIGN FOR THE PROSPECTUS OF "THE SAVOY"

ANOTHER DESIGN FOR THE PROSPECTUS OF "THE SAVOY"

COVER DESIGN
From "The Savoy," No. 1

CONTENTS PAGE
From " The Savoy," No. 1

THE ABBE
From " Under the Hill "

THE FOURTH TABLEAU OF "DAS RHEINGOLD"

ERDA
To Illustrate "Das Rheingold"

FLOSSHILDE
To Illustrate "Das Rheingold"

THE DEATH OF PIERROT

AVE ATQUE VALE: CATULLUS, CARMEN CI

AUBREY BEARDSLEY'S BOOK PLATE